19

African-American Heroes

Wynton Marsalis

Stephen Feinstein

Enslow Elementary

an imprint of

Enslow Publishers, Inc.

40 Industrial Road
Box 398
Berkeley Heights, NJ 07922
USA

http://www.enslow.com

Words to Know

classical music—A type of music invented in Europe hundreds of years ago by famous composers.

composing (com-POH-zing)—Writing music.

inspiration—Something that gives other people good ideas and feelings.

jazz—A type of music invented by African Americans. Musicians sometimes make up notes of their own when they play jazz.

Juilliard (JOO-lee-ard)—A famous music school in New York City.

musician (mew-ZIH-shun)—Someone who plays, sings, or writes music.

Enslow Elementary, an imprint of Enslow Publishers, Inc.

Enslow Elementary® is a registered trademark of Enslow Publishers, Inc.

Library of Congress Cataloging-in-Publication Data

Feinstein, Stephen.
 Wynton Marsalis / Stephen Feinstein.
  p. cm. — (African-American heroes)
 Includes index.
 ISBN-13: 978-0-7660-2766-4
 ISBN-10: 0-7660-2766-X
 1. Marsalis, Wynton—Juvenile literature. 2. Trumpet players—United States—Biography—Juvenile literature. [1. Marsalis, Wynton, 1961– 2. Trumpet players. 3. African Americans—Biography.] I. Title.
  ML3930.M327F45 2008
  788.9'2092—dc22
  [B]   2006034068

Printed in the United States of America

10 9 8 7 6 5 4 3 2 1

JUN 2 9 2007

To Our Readers: We have done our best to make sure all Internet Addresses in this book were active and appropriate when we went to press. However, the author and the publisher have no control over and assume no liability for the material available on those Internet sites or on links to other Web sites. Any comments or suggestions can be sent by e-mail to comments@enslow.com or to the address on the back cover.

Every effort has been made to locate all copyright holders of material used in this book. If any errors or omissions have occurred, corrections will be made in future editions.

Illustration Credits: AP/Wide World, pp. 1, 2, 3, 7, 12–13, 16, 17, 18, 19, 20, 21; Everett Collection, pp. 10 (upper right), 14 (right); EyeWire Images, p. 11; Deborah Feingold/Corbis, pp. 3, 14; Getty Images, pp. 5, 6, back cover; Lynn Goldsmith/Corbis, pp. 3, 15; Library of Congress, p. 10 (upper and lower left, lower right); Photos.com, pp. 3, 4, 8.

Cover Illustration: AP/Wide World.

Contents

Wynton Marsalis was born in New Orleans on October 18, 1961. Wynton's father, Ellis, and his mother, Dolores, loved music. Their favorite kind of music was **jazz**.

Ellis was a piano player who played in New Orleans jazz clubs. Ellis and Dolores hoped that their children would also become **musicians**. They named Wynton after a jazz piano player, Wynton Kelly.

Wynton Marsalis is one of the best trumpet players ever.

While Wynton was growing up, the house was always filled with the sounds of music. Wynton could hear people playing all over the house. Ellis would play the piano. Wynton's older brother, Branford, would be in a different room practicing the saxophone. Wynton's younger brother, Delfeayo, was learning to play the trombone. And his youngest brother, Jason, played the drums.

This picture shows, from left to right, Jason, Branford, Wynton, and their father, Ellis.

The famous trumpet player Al Hirt gave Wynton his first trumpet.

When Wynton was six, the well-known trumpet player Al Hirt gave him a trumpet. Wynton had his first trumpet lesson. But he was not really interested in learning how to play the trumpet. He did not want to spend hours a day practicing. Wynton would much rather play ball in the street with his friends.

Chapter 2
Wynton Learns How to Play the Trumpet

When Wynton was ten, he had his second trumpet lesson. But playing the trumpet was not easy for Wynton. He made funny sounds on the horn. Wynton knew that he would have to work hard if he wanted to get better. But Wynton still liked hanging out with his friends instead of practicing.

When Wynton was twelve, he had his third trumpet lesson. Now Wynton got serious about the trumpet. Ellis taught Wynton all about jazz music. He played records of the great jazz musicians for his son.

Wynton practiced three to five hours a day, playing his trumpet at every spare moment. Wynton began to learn how to play **classical music**.

Charlie Parker

Miles Davis

Dizzy Gillespie

Duke Ellington

Wynton liked to listen to records by great jazz musicians like these.

In high school, Wynton joined the band. He and his brother Branford played at dances with a couple of local groups. Wynton worked very hard on his trumpet and he kept getting better. He also worked hard in school. Wynton graduated from high school with very high grades.

Wynton enjoyed playing in the school band, like these students.

Chapter 3

Wynton Goes to New York

In 1979, at the age of eighteen, Wynton decided that he wanted to be a musician more than anything else. So he packed up his trumpet and went up north to New York City. There Wynton tried out for the **Juilliard** School of Music.

Juilliard is one of the most famous music schools in the world. Only the best music students can go there. When the teachers heard Wynton play, they chose him for the school.

These students are practicing at Juilliard. Wynton was one of the music students chosen to study there.

While at Juilliard, Wynton practiced the trumpet for many hours each day. He met musicians from all over the world. He learned about all different kinds of music. Wynton got a job in the evenings playing trumpet in a Broadway show. Then, in 1980, the jazz drummer Art Blakey asked Wynton to join his group, the Jazz Messengers.

Art Blakey was the leader of the Jazz Messengers.

The more Wynton practiced the trumpet, the better he became.

Wynton and Branford formed a new jazz band.

Wynton traveled all over the country playing with the Jazz Messengers. Art Blakey thought Wynton was one of the best jazz trumpet players he ever heard. He told Wynton to start his own band. So Wynton started a group with his brother Branford.

In 1982, Wynton made his first jazz record with the new band. It won a Grammy Award, an important music prize. In 1984, Wynton became the first person to ever win a Grammy for a jazz record and a Grammy for a classical record. The following year he won the same two awards again.

The Grammy Award looks like an old-fashioned record player.

Wynton Teaches Children About Jazz

Every year Wynton traveled to different cities to play jazz. He played in clubs and at concerts. Jazz was Wynton's favorite music because he could make up notes of his own as he played. Wherever he went, Wynton visited schools to teach children about jazz.

Wynton with high school musicians.

Wynton plays for students in Japan.

Wynton with fourth graders in New York City.

In 1991, Wynton became the director of the Jazz at Lincoln Center program in New York. There he organized jazz concerts. But Wynton enjoyed teaching just as much as performing. So in 1992, he started a series of educational programs for kids called Jazz for Young People. He did jazz programs on the radio and on TV. He wrote books about jazz, too.

In 2005, Hurricane Katrina hit the east coast of the United States. It destroyed many buildings in Louisiana, Mississippi, and Texas. The damage in New Orleans was terrible.

This made Wynton very sad, because New Orleans is his home town. So he played concerts to raise money and help the people of New Orleans rebuild their city.

Wynton tried to help the people who had been in Hurricane Katrina. In this picture, he is playing for children in New Orleans.

Wynton's Own Words

"Invest yourself in everything you do. There's fun in being serious."

Over the years, Wynton has brought joy to millions of music lovers. He has won many important prizes for **composing** and performing music.

Wynton has also been a great **inspiration** for young music students. He tells them there is only one way to improve their playing: practice, practice, practice!

Timeline

1961—Wynton is born in New Orleans on October 18.

1967—Wynton is given a trumpet and has his first trumpet lesson.

1979—Wynton starts studying music at the Juilliard School in New York City.

1980—Wynton joins Art Blakey's Jazz Messengers.

1982—Wynton starts a band with his brother Branford.

1991—Wynton becomes the director of Jazz at Lincoln Center in New York.

1992—Wynton starts the Jazz for Young People series at Lincoln Center.

1996—Wynton wins the Pulitzer Prize for music composition.

2005–2006—Wynton helps raise money for victims of Hurricane Katrina.

Learn More

Books

Burton, Marilee. *Artists at Work*. Philadelphia: Chelsea Clubhouse, 2003.

Ellis, Veronica Freeman. *Wynton Marsalis*. Austin, Texas: Raintree Steck-Vaughn, 1997.

Malone, Margaret Gay. *Jazz Is the Word: Wynton Marsalis*. New York: Marshall Cavendish Corp., 1998.

Web Sites

Academy of Achievement, "Wynton Marsalis"
<http://www.achievement.org>
 Go to "Select Achiever," then click on "Marsalis, Wynton."

"The Marsalis Family"
<http://www.sbgmusic.com>
 Go to "Teacher Support," then click on "Reference Articles," then "Performers," then "Marsalis Family."

Wynton Marsalis Official Web Site
<http://www.wyntonmarsalis.com>

Index